Can You Tell an Alligator from a Crocodile?

Buffy Silverman

Lerner Publications Company
Minneapolis

Lerner Publications Company
A division of Lerner Publishing Group, Inc.
241 First Avenue North
Minneapolis, MN 55401 U.S.A.

Website address: www.lernerbooks.com

Library of Congress Cataloging-in-Publication Data

Silverman, Buffy.
   Can you tell an alligator from a crocodile? / by Buffy Silverman.
      p.   cm. — (Lightning Bolt Books™—Animal look-alikes)
   Includes index.
   ISBN 978-0-7613-6733-8 (lib. bdg. : alk. paper)
   1. Alligators—Juvenile literature. 2. Crocodiles—Juvenile literature. I. Title.
QL666.C925S546 2012
597.98—dc22   2010050655

Manufactured in the United States of America
2 — CG — 4/1/12

Contents

Fat and Skinny Snouts

Alligators and crocodiles look a lot alike. They act alike too. But you can tell them apart.

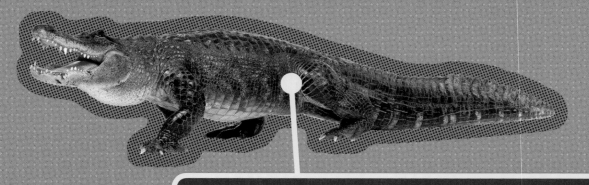

Alligators (above) and crocodiles (below) have many similarities. Can you spot the differences?

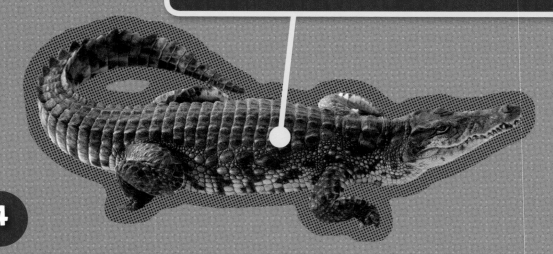

Look at this alligator's snout.
A snout is a kind of long nose.
An alligator's snout is shaped like the letter *U*.

The crocodile's snout is pointed. It looks like the letter *V*.

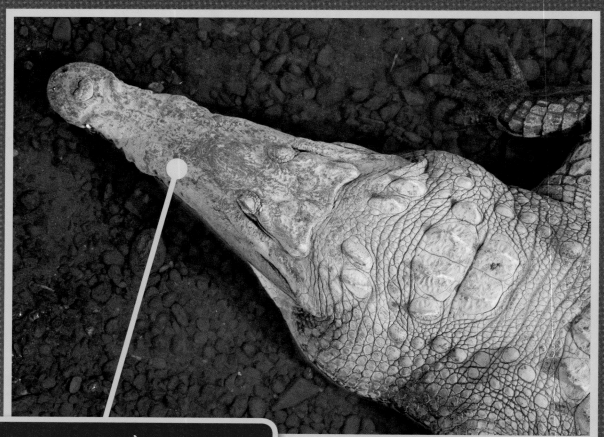

A crocodile's snout looks different from an alligator's.

An alligator's snout is wide and very strong. Alligators use their strong jaws to crush hard shells.

Look how wide this alligator can open its jaws!

A crocodile has a longer, narrow snout. A narrow snout is not as strong as a wide one. But a crocodile can still bite down hard. Its narrow snout is great for catching fish.

This crocodile catches a fish for a meal.

Toothy Grins

Alligators and crocodiles have sharp teeth. **You would not want to get close to them!**

An alligator shows off its sharp teeth.

This alligator's mouth is closed. You can see only its upper teeth. That's because an alligator's upper jaw is wider than its lower jaw. The lower teeth fit inside the upper jaw when its mouth is closed.

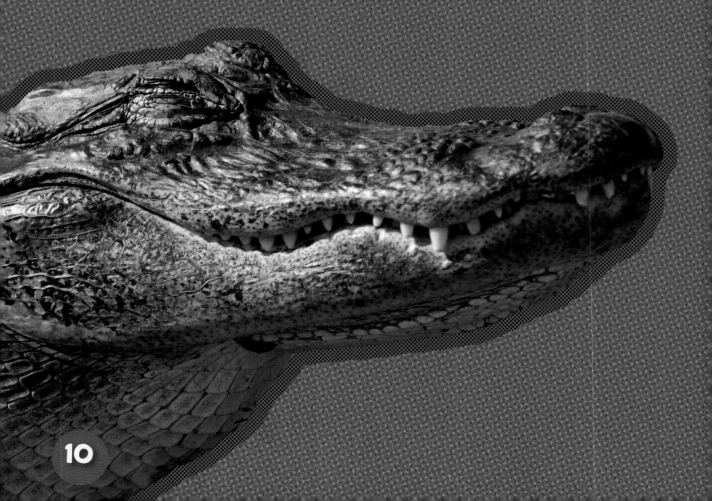

You can see a crocodile's upper and lower teeth. A crocodile's upper and lower jaws are the same size. The lower teeth fit along the upper jaw.

You can see both the upper and lower teeth of this crocodile. It almost looks like it is smiling.

Is the alligator about to catch this bird?

Alligators and crocodiles use their sharp teeth to hunt. The animals they catch are called their prey. Sometimes an alligator's or crocodile's teeth fall out when they catch their prey. Then new teeth grow in.

Sensing Others

Scales cover crocodiles' and alligators' skin. The scales have dark dots. These dots are sense organs.

The dots around this alligator's mouth are sense organs.

These sense organs can feel moving water. Moving water might mean that dinner is near.

Crocodiles have these
dots all over their bodies.
Alligators have them only
near their jaws.

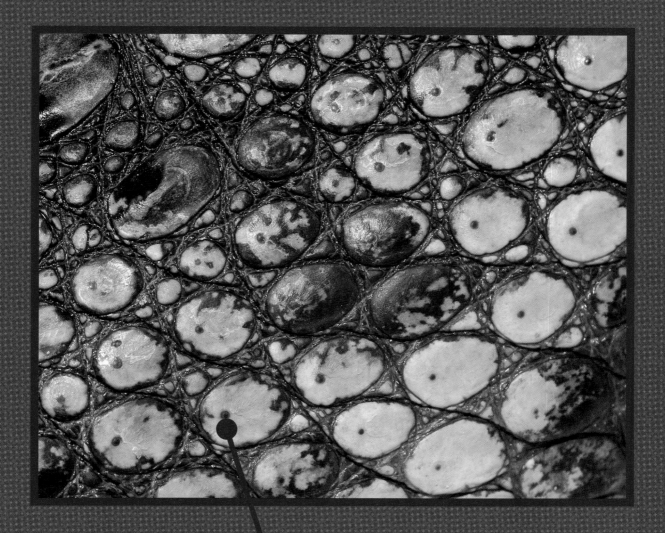

Dots like these cover
a crocodile's body.

Hungry Hunters

This alligator quietly waits in the water.

Crocodiles and alligators often lie still in water. You might think they are sleeping. But they are waiting.

This crocodile is floating in a swamp. It feels the water move. Its sense organs tell the crocodile that an animal is near.

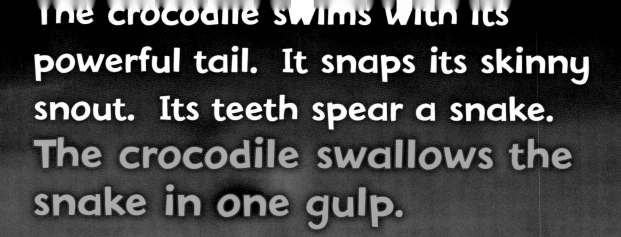

The crocodile swims with its powerful tail. It snaps its skinny snout. Its teeth spear a snake. **The crocodile swallows the snake in one gulp.**

Crocodiles also eat monkeys, deer, birds, fish, and other animals.

18

This hungry alligator lies in a marsh. Its eyes and nose poke above the water. It waits quietly, still as a floating log. The alligator senses something swimming near. A turtle paddles by.

The alligator swishes its giant tail. It lunges. Its wide snout snaps shut. It crushes the turtle's shell. The alligator swallows the turtle. Alligators also eat snails, crayfish, fish, birds, frogs, and other animals.

An alligator catches a large turtle for its next meal.

Alligators and crocodiles will
eat anything they catch.
They don't chew their food.
They swallow it
whole or tear
it into pieces.
Then they
gulp.

Watery Homes

Alligators and crocodiles live where there is water. They swim, dive, and float. Alligators usually swim in freshwater. Freshwater does not have a lot of salt in it. Rivers and most lakes are freshwater.

Crocodiles live near oceans.
Oceans have salt water.
Crocodiles swim where
freshwater and salt water mix.

This saltwater crocodile
swims in the South
Pacific Ocean.

Crocodiles have salt glands in their tongues. The glands get rid of salt. Alligators have glands too. But their glands do not get rid of salt. Alligators stay away from salt water.

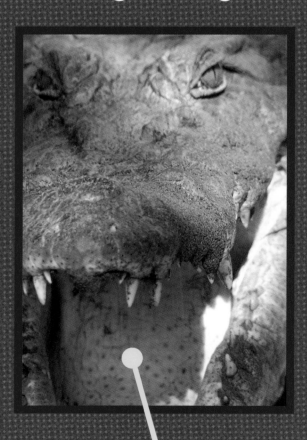

Compare the glands on the crocodile's tongue (left) to the glands on the alligator's tongue (right).

Alligators live only in North America, South America, and China. Crocodiles live in many places. They live in North America and South America. They also live in Africa, Asia, and Australia.

This animal lives in Botswana, a country in Africa. Is this an alligator or a crocodile?

Scientists think that crocodiles didn't always live in so many places. Scientists think crocodiles swam across oceans long ago. Their salt glands let them swim in salty oceans. The crocodiles found new homes.

Both alligators and crocodiles live and hunt in watery places.

Can you tell these look-alikes apart?

Who Am I?

Look at the pictures below. Which ones are alligators? Which ones are crocodiles?

I have a U-shaped snout.

My snout is pointed, like the letter *V*.

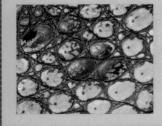

My skin has dots all over.

My skin is dotted only near my mouth.

My top and bottom teeth show when my mouth is closed.

Only my top teeth show when my mouth is closed.

Fun Facts

- Alligators and crocodiles lay eggs on land. They build nests that keep eggs warm. Alligators and crocodiles guard their nests from other animals.

- Alligator and crocodile babies cry inside their eggs. That tells their mom they will hatch soon.

- Mother alligators and crocodiles carry their new babies to water. They scoop them up in their mouths. Sometimes youngsters ride on their mom's back.

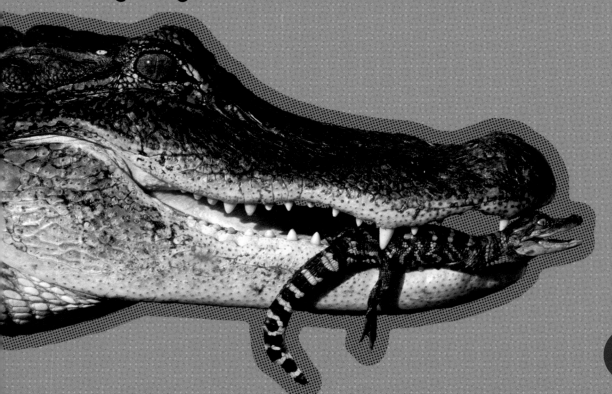

Glossary

freshwater: water that is not salty. Lakes, ponds, rivers, and streams that are away from the sea have freshwater.

prey: an animal that is hunted and eaten by other animals

salt gland: an organ that gets rid of extra salt

salt water: water that contains salt. Salt water is found near or in the sea.

scales: tough plates that cover and protect the skin of crocodiles, alligators, and other reptiles

sense organ: a special body part that helps an animal find out about its environment. Eyes and ears are sense organs. Alligators and crocodiles have sense organs in their skin.

snout: jaws or a nose that stick out from the front of an animal's head

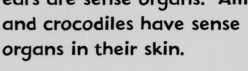

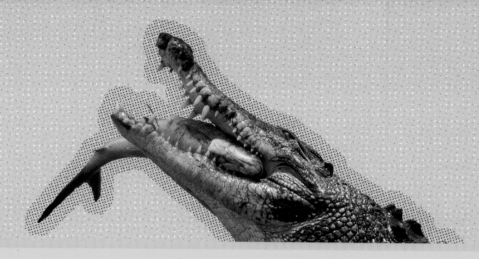

Further Reading

Gibbons, Gail. *Alligators and Crocodiles.* New York: Holiday House, 2010.

National Geographic Kids Creature Features: American Alligators
http://kids.nationalgeographic.com/kids/animals/creaturefeature/american-alligator

National Geographic Kids Creature Features: Nile Crocodiles
http://kids.nationalgeographic.com/kids/animals/creaturefeature/nile-crocodile

Photo Gallery: Alligators and Crocodiles
http://animals.nationalgeographic.com/animals/photos/alligators-and-crocodiles/#nile-crocodile_643_600x450.jpg

Pringle, Laurence. *Alligators and Crocodiles! Strange and Wonderful.* Honesdale, PA: Boyds Mills Press, 2009.

Silverman, Buffy. *Do You Know about Reptiles?* Minneapolis: Lerner Publications Company, 2010.

Index

Photo Acknowledgments

The images in this book are used with the permission of: © Stock Connection/
SuperStock, pp. 1 (top), 7; © Joel Sartore/National Geographic/Getty Images, p. 1
(bottom); © Chloe7992/Dreamstime.com, p. 2; © Eric Isselée/Dreamstime.com, pp. 4
(top), 9, 13, 28 (middle right); © Peter Hiscock/Dorling Kindersley/Getty Images, p. 4
(bottom); © age fotostock/SuperStock, pp. 5, 28 (top left); © James Caldwell/Alamy,
pp. 6, 28 (top right); © Stephen Noakes/Dreamstime.com, p. 8; © F1 ONLINE/SuperStock,
pp. 10, 28 (bottom right); © Fritz Polking/Visuals Unlimited, Inc., pp. 11, 28 (bottom left);
© Universal Stopping Point Photography/Flickr Select/Getty Images, p. 12; © Stu
Porter/Alamy, p. 14; © Raul Gonzalez Perez/Photo Researchers, Inc., pp. 15, 28 (middle
left); © Charles Krebs/Stone/Getty Images, p. 16; © Michael Stubblefield/Alamy, p. 17;
© David Curl/npl/Minden Pictures, p. 18; © Gerry Ellis/Digital Vision/Getty Images,
p. 19; © Larry Lynch/Alamy, p. 20; © Richard Du Toit/Minden Pictures, p. 21; © Eden
Batki/Botanica/Getty Images, p. 22; © Reinhard Dirscherl/Alamy, p. 23; © Nick Mott/
Dreamstime.com, p. 24 (left); © Image Quest Marine/Alamy, p. 24 (right);
© MicaWildlife/Alamy, p. 25; © Corbis/Alamy, p. 26; © Millard H. Sharp/Photo
Researchers, Inc., p. 27 (top); © Ben Cranke/Photodisc/Getty Images, p. 27 (bottom);
© Lockwood, C. C./Animals Animals, p. 29; © Yuriy Zelenen'kyy/Dreamstime.com,
p. 30; © ANT Photo Library/Photo Researchers, Inc., p. 31.

Front cover: © Steve Byland/Dreamstime.com (top); © Joel Sartore/National
Geographic/Getty Images (bottom).

Main body text set in Johann Light 30/36.